# A6M ZERO
## in action

by Shigeru Nohara 野原　茂
illustrated by Don Greer ドン・グリーア
& Shigeru Nohara 野原　茂

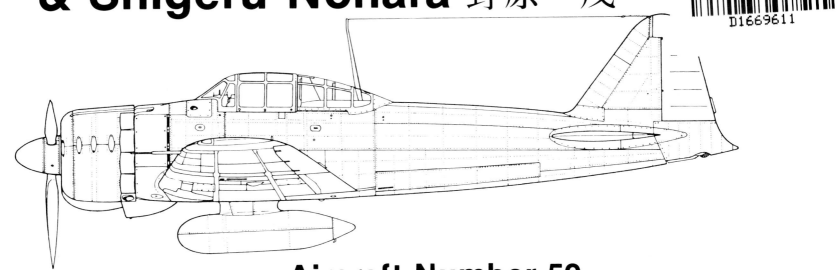

Aircraft Number 59

squadron/signal publications

A6M2 Model 21 off the HIRYU flown by Flight Leader Lt. Sumio during Operation Indian Ocean, April, 1942.

**COPYRIGHT © 1983 SQUADRON/SIGNAL PUBLICATIONS, INC.**

1115 CROWLEY DRIVE, CARROLLTON, TEXAS 75011-5010
All rights reserved. No part of this publication may be reproduced, stored in a retrival system or transmitted in any form by any means electrical, mechanical or otherwise, without written permission of the publisher.

**ISBN 0-89747-141-5**

If you have any photographs of the aircraft, armor, soldiers or ships of any nation, particularly wartime snapshots, why not share them with us and help make Squadron/Signal's books all the more interesting and complete in the future. Any photograph sent to us will be copied and the original returned. The donor will be fully credited for any photos used. Please send them to: Squadron/Signal Publications, Inc., 1115 Crowley Dr., Carrollton, TX 75011-5010.

## Photo Credits
## With thanks to:

| | |
|---|---|
| Ikuo Komori | Toshiharu Konada |
| Minoru Suzuki | F. Hino |
| Hirotoshi Maikuma | Yoshio Asaeda |
| Kimio Tanaka | Bonzi Matsumoto |
| Yonekichi Utsumi | Keizo Yamazaki |
| Takeo Tanimizu | Masaru Hagiwara |
| Takashi Miyake | Maru Magazine |
| Yoshio Sogawa | Takeshi Umemura |
| Hiroshi Tadano | Hatsutaro Tomura |

Leading a flight of Zeros during the Battle of Santa Cruz, Lt Hideki Shingo roars down the wooden deck of SHOKAKU. The tail of Shingo's A6M2 carries three White stripes on the tail which are outlined in Red and indicates that the plane belongs to a flight leader. EI-111 is also in Red.

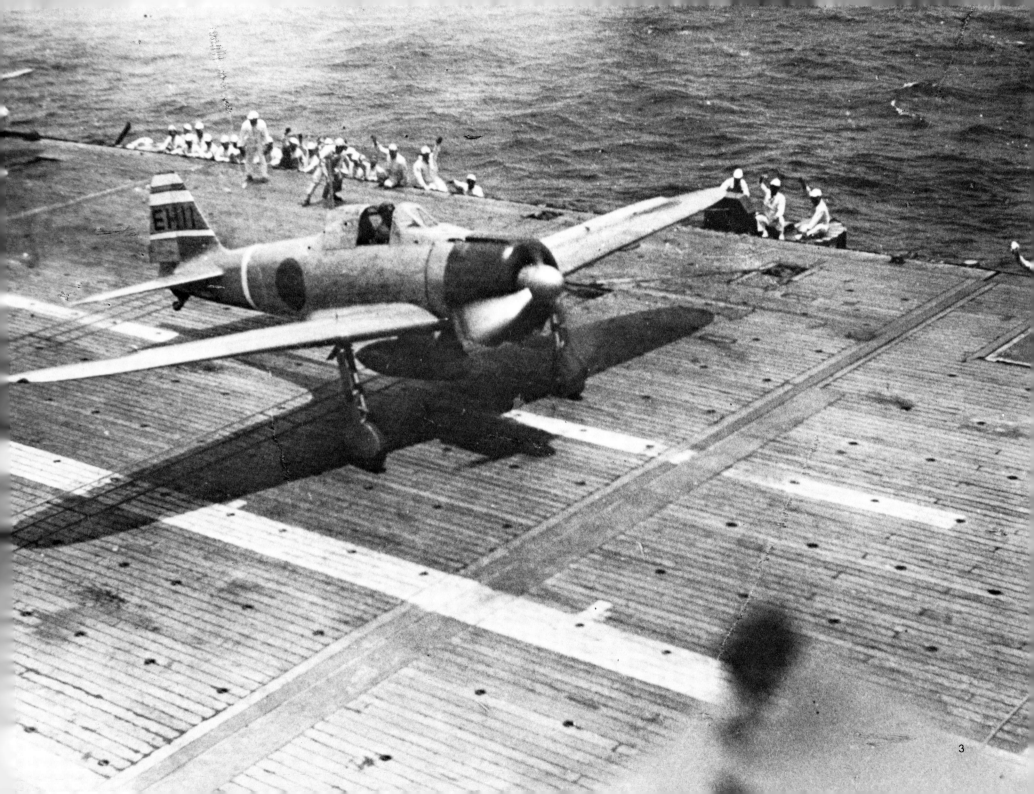

# Introduction

One of the most important factors influencing the Japanese military leadership in making the fateful decision to attack the United States and plunge Japan into the abyss of a war encompassing nearly the whole of the Pacific Ocean was the performance of the Zero Fighter.

At the time of its appearance, the Zero Fighter had a performance package far superior to any aircraft then in service or even on the drawing board of any other world power. Speed, range, rate of climb, manuverability, and the ability to operate from aircraft carrier decks combined to forge a seemingly invincible weapon in the hands of the Japanese Navy. A weapon that could be the cutting edge on the sword that Japan could use to dominate the Pacific. This vision proved to be irresistable to the military leadership and on the morning of 8 December 1941 (Japanese time) an air assault led by Zero Fighters was launched against the United States Pacific Fleet at Pearl Harbor.

In 1937, with Japanese forces moving ever deeper into China, and the possibility of a larger conflict with the United States over mineral rich Southeast Asia looming on the horizon, the Imperial Japanese Navy issued specifications to Mitsubishi and Nakajima for the development of an advanced "state of the art" fighter which would surpass the performance of any fighter aircraft it was likely to meet. Formally presented to the two aircraft companies on 17 January 1938 during a meeting at the Yokosuka Naval Air Arsenal, Nakajima, believing the specifications to be nearly impossible to meet withdrew from the competition. Mitsubishi however was persuaded to undertake development of the far reaching design specifications.

The Mitsubishi design team, led by Jiro Horikoshi, who had earlier led the design team for the very successful, but now becoming outdated, A5M, Type 96 carrier-borne Fighter (Claude), was immediately faced with powerplant selection. Three engines were available:

| Manufacturer | Mitsubishi | Mitsubishi | Nakajima |
| --- | --- | --- | --- |
| Name | Zuisei-13 | Kinsei-64 | Sakae-12 |
| Type | Radial | Radial | Radial |
| Cylinders | 14 | 14 | 14 |
| Horsepower | 875 | 1070 | 950 |
| Dry Weight | 526 kg | 560 kg | 530 kg |
| Diameter | 1118 mm | 1218 mm | 1150 mm |

But none were ideal. The *Sakae* 12 was rejected because it was manufactured by a competitor, and although favored, the 1070 hp *Kinsei* 64 was too heavy to meet the IJN's

**The A5M Type 96 carrier Fighter was also designed by Jiro Horikoshi, and is considered to be the forerunner of the Rei-sen, code named Claude by the Allies. The nimble little fighter was the backbone of the Navy fighter force until the introduction of the Zero. This A5M2a of the 13th Kokutai in China wears the standard Dark Green and Brown on the upper surfaces over Light Gray under surfaces. The fuselage band and tail number are in White. The large half egg shape on the belly of the A5M is an early type of drop tank.**

power loading requirements. Under the development designation 12-Shi, it was decided to build the airframe around the less powerful but lighter Zuisei 13.

With weight reduction being of prime importance most engineering innovations were directed to this end. The wing was built around a one piece main spar of Extra-Super Duralumium (ESD) which eliminated the need for heavy center section fittings. The Extra-Super Duralumium, a light weight aluminium alloy used for the first time in aircraft mainspar construction was similiar to the 24S aluminium used by the United States several years later. The fuselage center section was built as an integral part of the wing, which further saved weight as well as increasing ease of maintenance, and storage aboard aircraft carriers, since the front and rear sections of the fuselage were removable.

The long fuselage and large vertical tail provided excellent longitudinal and directional stability. The Mitsubishi 118 wing airfoil section along with a rather long wing span provided a wing loading as low as 21.5 lb/sq ft (105 kg/m2) in order to meet the Naval requirement of a landing speed of less than 66 mph (107 km/h) and still have the manuverability of the

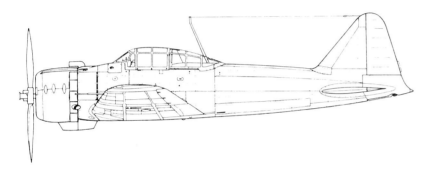

## 12-Shi (Experimental) Carrier Fighter

A5M Claude.

A pair of type 97 7.7MM machine guns were buried in the fuselage behind the cowling below the windscreen and fired through cowling troughs, the cocking mechanisms protruded into the cockpit through the instrument panel. A Swiss designed 20MM Oerlikon cannon, manufactured under license by the Dai-Nihon Heiki Company were mounted in each wing just outboard of the landing gear. Designated Type 99 Cannon, they were slightly slow in rate of fire and muzzle velocity but were extremely accurate and reliable.

The first 12-Shi prototype was rolled out on 16 March 1939 at the Mitsubishi plant in Southern Nagoya, but because there was no adjacent air strip the new fighter had to be dis-assembled, and transported twenty-five miles to Kagamigahara Airfield where it was re-assembled. On the afternoon of 1 April Mitsubishi test pilot, Katsuzo Shima, carried out initial taxi tests, and then rolling the 12-Shi down the runway, lifted off for a short jump flight before throttling back and settling back on to the runway. During the following days the testing program went smoothly, and except for a persistant unexplainable vibration in the engine and minor teething problems with the landing gear, results were excellent. Horikoshi had the two bladed propeller replaced with a constant speed three bladed propeller, the first constant speed propeller to be used on a Japanese aircraft. Flying with the new three bladed prop on 17 April the vibration in the 12-Shi's Zuisei 13 engine almost entirely disappeared. The first prototype carried out 119 flights logging 43 hrs. 26 mins. of air time.

By September 1939 the 12-Shi fighter had proven beyond any doubt that the design filled or exceeded the Imperial Japanese Navy's requirements, and on the 14th it was assigned it's military designation: A6M1 Type O carrier borne Fighter. The O was derived from the Japanese calender year 2600 (1940) in which the fighter was to enter service. Known as the Type O carrier borne Fighter which was Rei Shiki Sento Ki in the Japanese language, and was quickly shortened to Rei-sen*.

On 25 October 1939 a second prototype with improved elevator controls was delivered to the Navy's main test center at Yokosuka Air Base. No. 2 prototype began armament trials during late October and again results were better than expected. However on 11 March 1940, prototype No. 2 disintegrated in the air after an explosion, killing the test pilot. The origin of this tragedy has never been fully ascertained.

The decision was made to replace the Zuisei 13 engine with Nakajima's higher rated Sakae 12 engine. Flying for the first time on 18 January 1940 under the designation A6M2, No. 3 prototype with the more powerful Nakajima powerplant, exceeded all of the original IJN specifications. Before completion of test trials of the third and fourth prototypes, the Navy Air Force in China, hearing of the Rei-sen's performance, began clamoring for it. On 21 July, ten days before the Rei-sen was officially accepted into regular Naval service, and over the objections of Mitsubishi engineers, fifteen preproduction machines were sent to the 12th Kokutai (12th Air Corps) at Hankow. On 19 August Lt Tamotsu Yokoyama led the first Rei-sen formation into combat when 54 G3M2 Nells were escorted to Chungking. Unfortunately no opposition was met. The next day was the same. It was not until the Rei-sen's fourth mission that first blood was drawn. On 13 September, again having escorted bombers to Chungking, the Rei-sens were leaving the area when Russian built Chinese Air Force I-15 and I-16 fighters were spotted converging on the smoking target. Turning, the Japanese pilots climbed for height and dove on the luckless Chinese pilots. In the ensuing melee all 27 Chinese aircraft were shot down without loss to the Japanese. From 19 August 1940 to the end of the year, 153 Rei-sen sorties were flown, 59 Chinese aircraft were claimed as aerial kills and 101 on the ground; no Rei-sen loss was recorded. This initial training ground over China led the Japanese to believe that the Rei-sen was nearly invincible. The Chinese also believed it and allowed A6M2 escorted bombers to range over China unmolested. General Claire L. Chennault commander of the Flying Tigers tried to warn Washington of the Zero's capabilities, but was ignored.

While at Hankow the Sakae 12 cooling problem was solved. However, the drop tank's reluctance to seperate above 200 mph would plague the Rei-sen for sometime.

Production of the Rei-sen began at the Mitsubishi Nagoya plant under the designation A6M2 Type O Model 11 carrier borne Fighter, with the first production machine rolling out during December 1939, the first of over 10,000 Rei-sens to be produced during the next five years of war. It is interesting to note that the Rei-sen's engine never exceed 1200 hp, even in the final production version. And yet, as the war progressed the Rei-sen was called upon to battle fighters powered by engines in excess of 2000 hp. The Rei-sen weighed 25% less than the F4F Wildcat and was less than half the weight of the F6F Hellcat.

One of the reasons for this lightness was the lack of armor plate protection for the pilot and fuel tanks. Japanese military philosophy and tradition honored only the attack, the additional weight for armored defense even to protect the life of a very expensively trained pilot was abhorent to a military tradition of 100 years. Some Rei-sen pilots regularly flew combat missions without a parachute to further reduce weight.

The phenomenal range of the Rei-sen (1875 miles) using a drop tank, which also was a Rei-sen production first, was also a big contributor to the Zero legend. Japanese pilots received special training in how to fly at the most economical speed in order to increase the Rei-sen's range and arrive in the combat area with enough fuel to engage in lengthy combats. The Rei-sen flew far and wide over the Pacific, and with the fighter popping up everywhere the allies estimated Zero strength at several times its actual numbers.

*During the war the A6M was popularly known as the Rei-sen among the Japanese, but since the end of the war the Japanese word Rei has been popularly replaced by the English word Zero, coining the combination English/Japanese word Zero-sen. Throughout the rest of the world the A6M has always been known as the Zero. In the text of this book we will be using the terms Rei-sen and Zero interchangeably.

# Developments
## A6M Type 0 Carrier Fighter

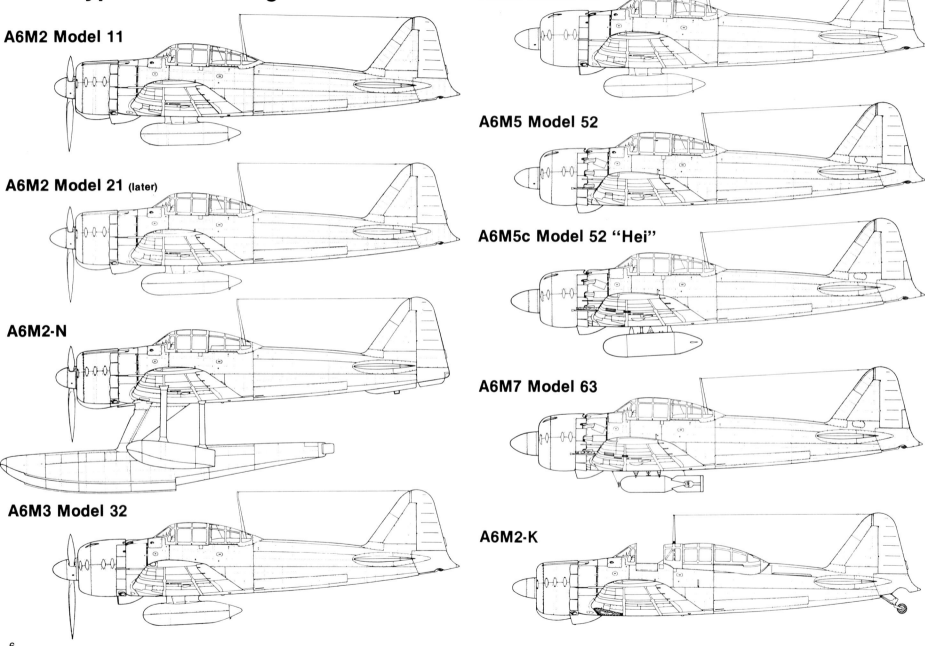

A6M2 Model 11

A6M2 Model 21 (later)

A6M2-N

A6M3 Model 32

A6M3 Model 22

A6M5 Model 52

A6M5c Model 52 "Hei"

A6M7 Model 63

A6M2-K

# A6M2 Model 11

On 14 September when the 12-*Shi* was officially accepted and given the military designation A6M, the *Zuisei* 13 powered 1st and 2nd 12-*Shi* prototypes were given the designation A6M1. The *Sakae* 12 powered aircraft, including No. 3 and No. 4 prototypes, and the fifteen preproduction machines sent to China were designated A6M2 Model 11. The total number of Model 11s built would be 64 machines (No. 3 through No. 67).

The introduction of the *Sakae* 12 engine neccessitated a redesign of the carburetor intake which was moved to the lower front of the cowling just below the spinner and became an integral part of the cowling. The large oil cooler intake was replaced by a smaller and more streamlined intake that just overlapped the bottom of the cowling. The exhaust pipes, which had exited through the fourth cowl flap position on the *Zuisei* powered 12-*Shi* machines, initially exited through the fifth cowling flap position on *Sakae* powered Model 11. However, overheating problems caused a redesign of the exhaust collector ring with the exhaust pipe being moved back to the fourth flap position. Several minor changes were affected on the assembly line. The greenhouse glass panels just behind the radio mast were shortened and the back was faired over with metal, this change being affected from aircraft No. 47. The recessed cannon aperture was made flush with the leading edge, and the small air inlet on the leading edge near the fuselage was reduced in diameter.

Most of the Model 11s were sent to land-based Naval squadrons in China, approximately 30 were assigned to the 12th *Kokutai* in central China, and 9 to the 14th *Kokutai* in southwest China. Even with so few Zeros available, the new aircraft's range and performance allowed the Japanese Imperial Navy to totally dominate the skies over China. By August of 1941 Zeros had claimed some 266 enemy aircraft in the air and on the ground. Only two *Rei-sens* were recorded as being lost to enemy action and these were brought down by flak.

General Chenanault repeatedly reported the presence and performance of the new Japanese "super fighter", and repeatedly he was ignored.

KA-103, has the exhaust pipes exiting through the fifth cowl flap position next to the oil cooler intake. Overheating caused this arrangement to be revised with the exhaust pipe being moved to the fourth cowl flap position on later Model 11s. This machines also has the recessed cannon apperture and the large cockpit air intake in the leading edge of wing. Note the landing gear position indicater stick silouetted against the sky just above the port landing gear.

KA-103, an early Model 11 assigned to the Kasumigaura (Training) Kokutai prepares for take off. The aircraft is painted overall Light Gray with Yellow/Orange IFF stripes on the leading edge of both wings. The Black anti-glare panel rather than a full Black cowling is very unusual for a Zero.

## Cowling Development

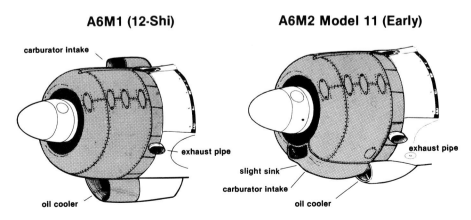

A6M1 (12-Shi)  |  A6M2 Model 11 (Early)

This early Model 11 has the number 433 and a slogan of patriotism denoting that the aircraft was donated by a civil organization painted on the side of the fuselage. 433 identifies the donation, not the aircraft. All letters and numbers are in Black.

Flying over Hankow, China, No. 3-177 an A6M2 Model 11 of the 12th Kokutai carries a Red fuselage band and tail stripe. Tail and fuselage bands on aircraft of the 12th, were in Blue, Yellow or Red, depending on the flight.

No. 3-182 of the 12th Kokutai carries a Yellow fuselage band. For some unknown reason this machine has been painted in at least two shades of gray.

## A6M2 Model 11 (Late)

### Cowling

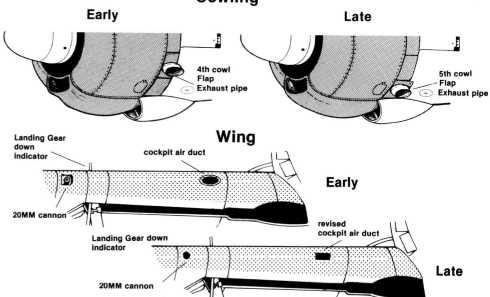

Early — 4th cowl Flap / Exhaust pipe

Late — 5th cowl Flap / Exhaust pipe

### Wing

Early — Landing Gear down indicator, cockpit air duct, 20MM cannon

Late — Landing Gear down indicator, revised cockpit air duct, 20MM cannon

This pair of Model 11s of the 12th Kokutai are heading toward enemy targets deep in China on 26 May 1941. No. 3-136 is flown by Naval Air Pilot 3/C Kunimori Nakakariya (16 victories) and 3-141 is flown by flight leader Lt Miroru Suzuki. Aircraft 3-136, an early Model 11, seems to have the long greenhouse glass panels behind the radio mast found on Model 11s prior to production No. 47.

All the fuselage bands are Blue, with the flight leader, Lt Suzuki's aircraft carrying two Blue fuselage bands. The nearest aircraft carries a single Red tail stripe, the second machine a pair of White tail stripes and the third machine a pair of Blue tail stripes, all of which denote that the aircraft belong to different flights within the 12th Kokutai.

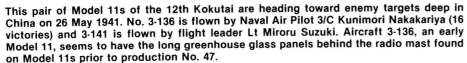

A very interesting data plate which carries the following information:

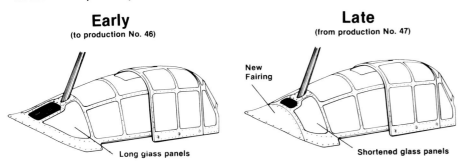

| Type | 12 Shi (Experimental) Carrier Fighter |
|---|---|
| Manufacturing Number | Mitsubishi No. 807 |
| Manufacturing Date | 0 - 5 - 1 |
| Assigned | |

The production number 807 is obviously to deceive the enemy if the aircraft happens to fall into their hands. The actual production number is believed to be No. 7, with the actual date of manufacture being 0-5-1, meaning 1 May 2600 (1940). The aircraft, an A6M2 Model 11, flown by Lt M. Suzuki, carriers a Red fuselage band and a Blue tail stripe. The 28 kill markings, swallows inside a circle, are the total victories of Lt Suzuki and the previous pilot.

# A6M2 Model 21

The earlier A6M2 Model 11 had performed extremely well during aircraft carrier trials conducted aboard SORYU during June of 1940. But while the Zero's performance aboard the carrier was excellent, the fighters long wing span constantly ran the risk of wing tip damage while going up and down on the carriers' elevators. The problem was solved by providing 20 inch wingtip panels that could be manually folded upwards. Designated A6M2 Model 21, a further production line change was introduced on aircraft No. 127 when the aileron balance was changed. The new aileron balance system was linked to the landing gear retraction system and considerably improved high speed control by reducing the amount of force needed to move the control stick.

In addition to the Mitsubishi production line at Nagoya, Nakajima (a much larger concern than Mitsubishi) was instructed to begin production of the Model 21. With Nakajima beginning production during November of 1941, 740 Model 21 fighters would be built before production terminated

By the late fall of 1941 nearly 400 *Rei-sen* fighters had been delivered to the Imperial Navy Air Force. The carrier force was equipped with 126 Zeros and the land based squadrons 213. The Navy's superbly trained pilots were confident that they could master any enemy met. The Japanese Imperial Navy Air Force at this time was quite possibly the strongest and most effective air force in the world. It has been pointed out that if the Luftwaffe had possessed the Zero during the Battle of Britain, history might have taken a much different course.

*If the Messerschmitt Bf 109 had more fighting radius during the Battle of Britain, at least half the range of the Zero — the Zero could cover all of Britain from the German bases in France — the history of Europe would have been quite different.*

As strong as the Japanese Navy Air Force had become and as openly as it had been tested and used during the previous year in China — its existance would come as a near total surprise to the United States. Japan's military leadership, however, was well aware of its strength and by the fall of 1941 this strength proved irresistable. The HAWAIIAN OPERATION (Attack on Pearl Harbor) was approved. It should be noted that the attack on the United States Pacific Fleet was not planned by the Japanese to be a "sneak attack" but as a surprise attack after war had been declared. However the Japanese embassy staff was unable to decode and deliver the declaration of war prior to the actual attack.

(Upper Right) An A6M2 Model 21 with its wing tips folded is being transferred from a harbor barge to a transport. This machine carries a White outlined Hinomaru, which is very rarely seen on a Light Gray aircraft. The Red outlined 'no step' area can be seen on the rear of the wing near the wing root.

The large aileron mass balance counter weight can be seen on the lower side of the aileron. These were replaced with a system linked to the landing gear retraction system which considerably improved handling at high speeds, and was put into production on aircraft No. 127.

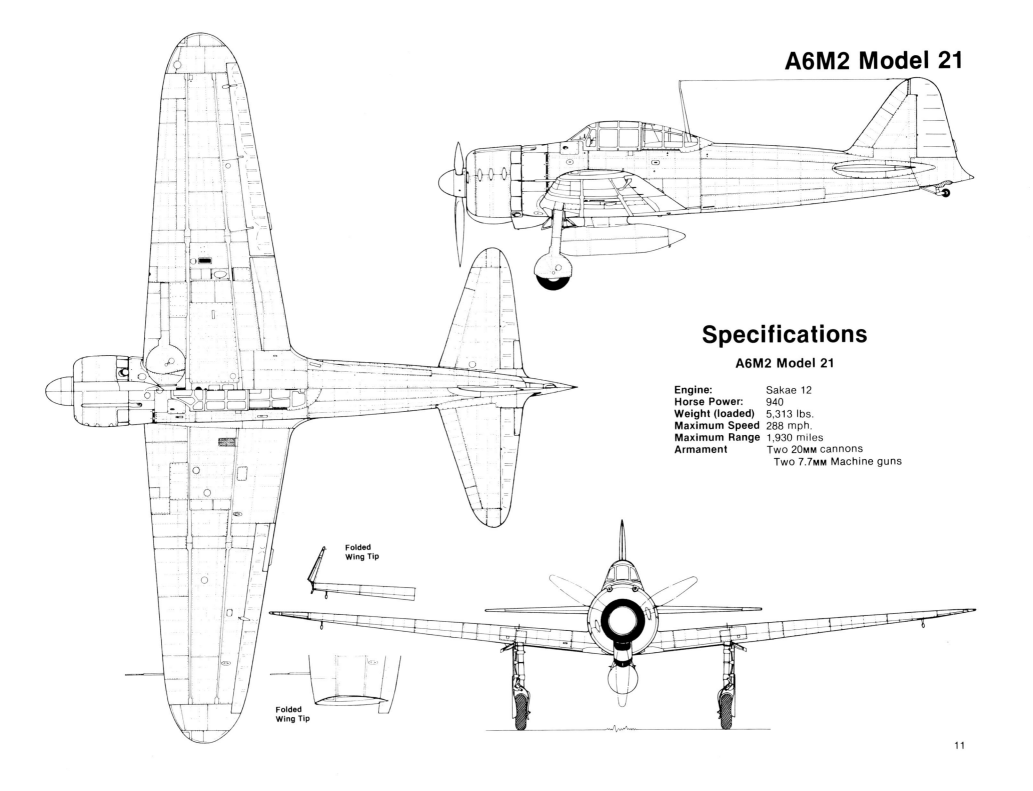

AI-156, an early A6M2 Model 21 is tied down on the deck of AKAGI at Hitocap Bay on the northeastern coast of Japan, from which the Hawaiian Operation (Pearl Harbor Attack) Task Force sailed. Note that the last two digits of the aircraft code is repeated on the front edge of the cowling in White and on the landing gear cover in Black.

(Above Right) This A6M2 Model 21, on the deck of AKAGI as she nears Hawaii, carries a single Red fuselage band and tail codes AI-105 in Black with a Yellow/Orange stripe above and below the codes. AI-101 in the background belongs to the 1st Koku Sentai (Carrier Air Division) flight leader, Major Sigeru Itaya.

## Model 21 Folding Wing Tip

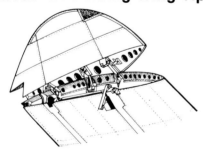

At 6 am on the morning of 8 December (Japanese time) 183 planes of the first attack wave were launched from the wooden flight decks toward Hawaii. Within hours the United States Pacific Fleet virtually ceased to exist. However two aircraft carriers, LEXINGTON and ENTERPRISE, were at sea and were unharmed. Had Admiral Nagumo launched a second attack it very well might have caught the American carriers on their arrival at Pearl Harbor, Admiral Nagumo refused. This was a mistake that the Imperial Navy would pay dearly for during the coming months.

# Carrier Air Group
## Markings April 1941-June 1942

EII-111, a Zero 21, roars off the deck of the ZUIKAKU during the January 1942 taking of Rabaul. The double white fuselage ID stripes of the ZUIKAKU can be seen painted on the fuselage, the data plate has not been overpainted.

EII-140 awaits the launch signal from the control officer. The last two digits of the aircraft code are painted on the carburetor air scoop. The second aircraft carries the numeral 45 on the scoop.

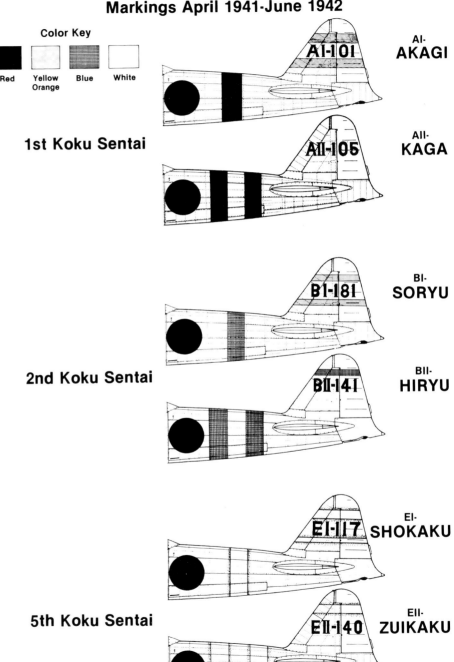

Part of Vice Admiral Takagi's Strike Force, ZUIKAKI, her flight deck covered with aircraft, is seen steaming toward the Coral Sea to support the invasion force heading to Port Moresby. The Battle of the Coral Sea was the first true carrier battle with all the action taking place without the surface ships ever sighting each other. The Japanese lost the light carrier SHOHO, and SHOKAKU was damaged. The U.S. lost the LEXINGTON and the YORKTOWN was damaged. The Japanese Navy had heavy losses of experienced pilots.

## TAIL WHEEL
Retraction Mechanism

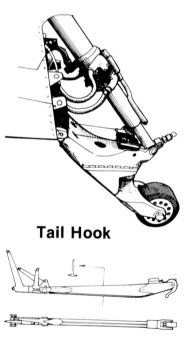

### Tail Hook

On 26 October 1942 (Japanese time), the SHOKAKU prepares to launch her planes against USS ENTERPRISE during the Battle of Santa Cruz. At the extreme right is EI-111 belonging to the flight leader Lt Hideki Shingo. ENTERPRISE was hit and damaged but her speed was unimpaired and she was able to retire, HORNET however had to be abandoned. U.S. dive bombers attacked and seriously damaged SHOKAKU, but more importantly, more than one hundred experienced Japanese pilots were lost.

X-183, of the 23rd Hikotai at Ambon Island, has had the radio equipment removed. Since the radios experienced a very low degree of reliability and replacement parts were very difficult to obtain, pilots often had the radio equipment removed to save additional weight.

X-182 carries a Red band on the fuselage and a Red stripe on the tail. An earlier Red band on the fuselage has been over painted.

## Main Landing Gear

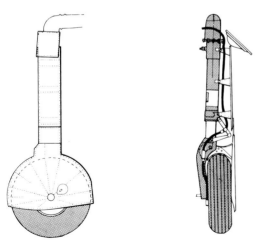

X-183, an A6M2 Model 21, flown by Naval Air Pilot 2/C Yoshiro Hashiguchi of the 23rd Hikotai (3rd Kokutai), carries 11 Redish Pink cherry blossom kill markings on the fin. The stripes above the kill markings are White and the rudder appears to be Red.

Zero 21s lined up at Rabaul East during the summer of 1943. The 'I' marking has not been identified.

(Below) Zero 21s from ZUIKAKU are seen at Rabaul during 1943 while helping to cover the withdrawl of Japanese troops from Guadalcanal. Each of the aircraft is marked with a single White fuselage band outlined in Red. In front of the present fuselage band is evidence of an earlier White band having been over painted. (Aircraft assigned to ZUIKAKU had earlier been identified with two White fuselage bands.)

The Tainan Kokutai at Rabaul during the summer of 1942. On 9 December 1941 (Japanese time), the day after the Hawaiian Operation, the Tainan Kokutai flew the 1,125 miles from Formosa to the Philippines escorting bombers, and together with the bombers, destroyed Clark Air Base and some 65 American Fighters. HOKOKU-535 on the fuselage indicates that the plane was donated by a civil organization. Note that both aircraft are without radio masts.

During 'Operation I-GO', the Japanese counter attack on Guadalcanal, Zeros were staged from the main airfield at Rabalul to Buin, an advanced air base on Bougainville. These A6M2 Model 21s with Dark Green splotches over the Light Gray are believed to be of the 204th Kokutai.

## Port Wheel Well

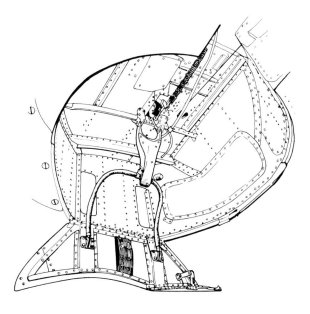

Aircraft in the Solomon's area had been unofficially wearing the additional Dark Green paint since the summer of 1942, it was not until April 1943 that this scheme was adopted officially. Admiral Yamamoto was on his way to Buin when his aircraft was shot down and he was killed on 18 April 1943.

In November of 1943, the 1st Koku Sentai off ZUIKAKU was flown into Buin to help support "Operation RO-GO" when U.S. forces landed on Bougainville. The third aircraft in the line up is an A6M3 Model 22. The White chevron on the aircraft are the markings of ZUIKAKU.

(Above) This A6M2 Model 21, O-TA-150 of the Oita (Training) Kokutai, carries an unusual Black nose that extends beyond the cowling up to the fire wall; the wheel well covers are also painted Black. The spinner is Red tipped in Yellow/Orange while the propeller blades are polished metal with a single Red line on the tip of each prop. The aircraft number on the tail is imposed on a White band and the aircraft number is repeated on the under surface of the port wing. This machine has had the tail cone removed.

This Zero 21 of the Tsukuba (Training) Kokutai carries an aircraft number in the 300s which was reserved for the use of attack fighters. Also unusual is the use of a White outline on the wing Hinomaru while the fuselage national insignia is without a White outline — the reverse of official regulations.

This Zero 21, coded I-HA-109, belonging to the Iwakuni Kokutai, has the 9 repeated on the landing gear cover and carburetor intake. Note the larger type spinner that was introduced on the A6M3 and has been retrofitted to this Model 21.

**(Left)** These Zero 21s neatly lined up on the flightline, belong to the Oita (Training) Kokutai and carry four digit tail numbers because there are several different types of aircraft in the group. The White line on the fuselage is for attitude confirmation.

**(Lower Left)** Ground crew of the Oita (Training) Kokutai carry out engine maintainence on a Model 21's Sakae 12 powerplant. The aircraft code, O-TA-111, being carried on the undersurface of the wing is not unusual for training aircraft.

**(Below)** This Model 21, belonging to the Oita (Training) Kokutai, has a crudely painted White identification line on the wing, while the Zero in front has the entire horizontal tail surfaces painted White. Some aircraft had the nose painted White.

(Above) YO-101, an A6M2 Model 21 special training aircraft used for training pilots to fly the rocket powered Mitsubishi J8M1 'Shusui' intercepter, which was developed from a technical manual (a sample aircraft and the detailed drawings had been destroyed enroute) of the German Messerschmitt Me 163 Komet that were brought from Germany by submarine.

## Type 98 Gun Sight

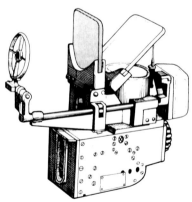

(Above Left) Zero 21s of Tsukuba (Training) Kokutai have had both wheel covers and tail cones removed. The vertical and horizontal lines behind the Hinomaru are in White. The demarcation line between the Dark Green upper surfaces and the Light Gray under surfaces is wavy.

(Left) These aircraft belonging to the 302nd Kokutai at Atsugi during 1945 are part of the Home Defense. Each of the three Zero 21s carry a somewhat different camouflage scheme. The last aircraft is a J2M1 Raiden intercepter.

# A6M3 Model 32

To increase the high altitude performance of the A6M *Rei-sen,* a 1,130 hp *Sakae* 21 engine with a two speed supercharger was installed under the designation A6M3 Model 32. A completely redesigned, more rounded and slightly larger cowling was fitted over the larger powerplant. A larger propeller and spinner were installed. The *Sakae* 21 engine had a downdraft carburetor so the air scoop was moved from the bottom front of the cowling to the top front. The exhaust collector was redesigned and the exhaust pipes were relocated from exiting through the fourth cowling flap to exiting through the fifth cowling flap position.

To help reduce the increase in weight brought about by the installation of the more powerful engine and to increase maneuverability at high speeds the 20 inch folding wing tips were removed and faired over, creating squared wing tips. Reducing the wing span by over three feet and increasing the engine power did not bring about the anticipated increase in performance. The Model 32 was only slightly more manueverable at high speeds, maximum speed was increased by less than 2 miles per hour and roll characteristics had improved only a little; climb rate was slightly decreased, and turning radius was slightly increased. The *Sakae* 21 engine consumed very little more fuel at cruise speed than the *Sakae* 12 engine, however, the *Sakae* 21's fuel consumption during full power and a 21 gallon reduction in fuel capacity served to reduce the Model 32's range considerably. Ammunition for the type 99 20MM cannon was increased from 60 rounds per gun to 100 rounds per gun.

The initial flight trials of the A6M3 Model 32 were carried out during June of 1941. The first unit to receive the new fighter being the 2nd *Kokutai* during the spring of 1942. Operating in the New Guinea area, the Model 32's short range prevented the 2nd *Kokutai* from reaching the battle over Guadalcanal during its early stages. Other units received the Zero 32, mainly in the Solomons area, but the new fighter was not well received by front line units and most of the 343 Model 32s produced by Mitsubishi were relegated to the training role in Japan.

Initially this squared wing aircraft was code named "Hap" in honor of Air Force General "Hap" Arnold, however General Arnold, feeling less than honored, ordered the code name changed to "Hamp". In December of 1942 the code name was revised to Zeke 32 after examples had been examined.

**The rounded, slightly bulbous appearing, new cowling housing the 1,130 hp Sakae 21 engine enclosed the gun troughs within the cowling. The 7.7 machine guns fired through elongated slits in the top front of the cowling. The new position of the carburetor air scoop can be seen just behind the upper propeller blade. These Light Gray machines with Black cowlings belong to the Iwakuni Kokutai.**

## Cowling Development

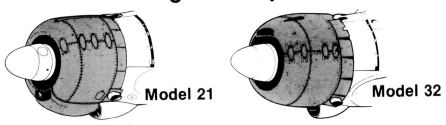

Model 21     Model 32

**The deletion of the 20 inch folding wing tips and the addition of wing tip fairings created a squared clipped looking wing tip on the Model 32. The new spinner was slightly larger and more rounded than the Zero 21 and the propeller blades were longer than the blades on the Zero 21. The Black paint applied to the cowlings was not a true Black but actually a Blue-Black.**

Q-122, a Zero 32 of the 2nd Kokutai taking off from Rabaul East, carries a Blue fuselage band denoting a section leader. Note that this machine is without a radio mast. A twin engine Nakajima J1N1-R type 2 long range Reconnaissance aircraft (Irving) is in the background.

Rabaul East covered with Zero 32s of the 2nd Kokutai during August of 1942. The G4M Betty Bomber (Q-901) was used as a "hack" aircraft by the 2nd.

The 2nd Kokutai was the first combat unit to be equipped with the A6M3 Model 32. The aircraft taking off in the background is an Army Mitsubishi Type 100 Reconnaissance aircraft in use by the Navy.

## Wing Development

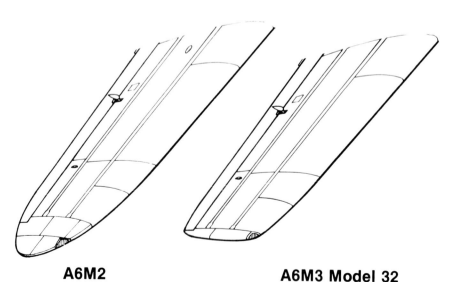

A6M2          A6M3 Model 32

T2-190, an A6M3 Model 32 of the 204th Kokutai at Rabaul during the summer of 1943. This machine is Light Gray overall with Dark Green splotches very heavily smeared on the upper surfaces. In the Solomon's it became unusual to see a Zero that was not over painted with Dark Green. The tail code "T" was used by the 204th from late 1942 until the summer of 1943.

An A6M3 Model 32 preparing for a night mission, the clipped wing tips are clearly visible.

A formation of Zero 32s of the Tsukuba (Training) Kokutai. The White line on the fuselage and tail were aids for flight training.

The Sakae 21 engine of the A6M3 Model 32 is being run up prior to takeoff. The lack of a gunsight indicates that this is probably a training aircraft. The camouflage is the standard late scheme of Dark Green upper surfaces over Light Gray lower surfaces. The White outline on the national insignia is the specified 75mm in width.

# A6M3 Model 22

Early in 1942 it was decided to restore the 20 inch wing tips and folding mechanisms to the *Sakae* 21 powered model, along with the addition of 12 gallon fuel tanks in each wing. Under the designation A6M3 Model 22 the new series was put into production during the fall of 1942. The Model 22 had actually preceded the Model 32 in design concept, but had been put off while the Model 32 was developed. Very early in the Zero 22s production run the rudder trim tab was recessed into the rudder.

Performance of the Model 22 was superior to the earlier 32, and the range of the Model 22 was the longest of all the Zero Models, being 100 miles greater than even the Model 21. As the fighting on Guadalcanal raged, the Zero 22 was rushed to Buna in New Guinea and Buka in the Solomon Islands to provide cover over the supply route to Guadalcanal. While most Zero 22s were land based, it is known that this model served on board the ZUIKAKU.

# A6M3a Model 22a

Late production Model 22s, under the designation A6M3 Model 22KO* (A6M3a Model 22a), were armed with the long barrelled Type 99 Model 2-3 20MM cannon with a higher muzzle velocity. A few of the Model 22s were fitted with an experimental 30MM cannon and operationally tested at Rabaul. 560 A6M3 Model 22s were produced by Mitsubishi between the fall of 1942 and the summer of 1943.

## Wing Development

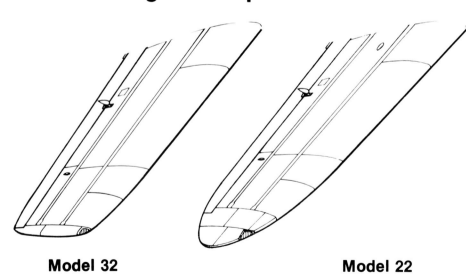

Model 32          Model 22

*In the Japanese language KO, OTSU, and HEI are similiar to the English equivilents of A,B,C, or first, second, third, and are often used to denote sub-types.

The round folding wing tips were added back to the Model 22, creating the longest ranged Zero of them all. I-HA-159, a Zero 22 of the Iwakuni (Training) Kokutai during mid 1943, on which the camouflage extends right to the underside of the fuselage. The basic undercarriage retraction system design, which was first used on the Nakajima Type 97 Carrier Attack Bomber was a refinement of the system used on the Vought 143. This and other system designs that were similiar or copies of systems found in other aircraft designs was the basis for the wartime propaganda that the Zero was a poor copy of a rejected U.S. aircraft design. This may have been good propaganda, but factually it was pure rubbish. The Zero was as original as any other aircraft design of World War II.

A6M3 Model 22 Rei-sen of the 1st Koku Sentai off the ZUIKAKU at Rabaul as part of operation "RO-GO" during November of 1943. The Zero 22 with the two White chevrons is believed to belong to the commander of ZUIKAKU's fighter force. All tail markings have been deleted by the wartime censor.

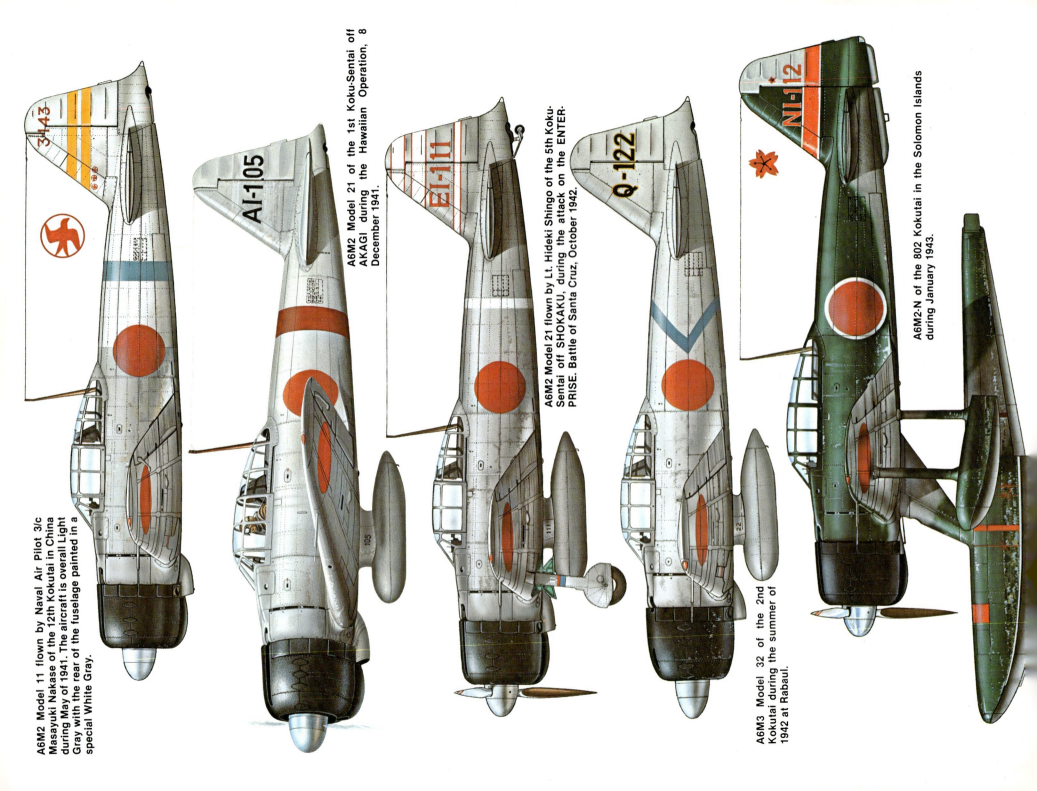

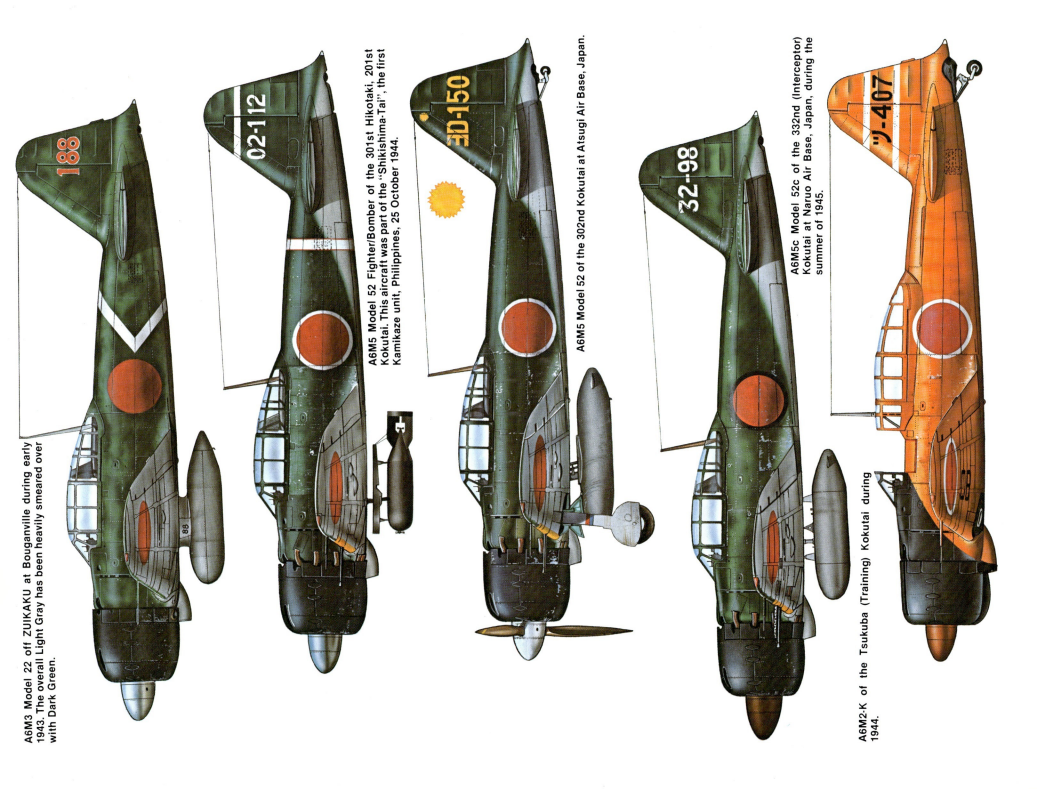

These Zero 22s of the Iwakuni (Training) Kokutai carry the overall Light Gray scheme. The new recessed rudder trim tab is the large dark area at the rear bottom of the rudder.

A6M3 Model 22s of an unknown unit at Rabaul in late 1943. The center aircraft, coded 7-101, carries two Yellow/Orange diagonal fuselage bands and is believed to belong to the unit commander. Each aircraft has had its landing gear covers removed. The revetment is made of earth filled fuel drums.

A line up of Zero 22s of the Iwakuni (Training) Kokutai, framed below the folded wing tip of another Model 22.

## Rudder Development

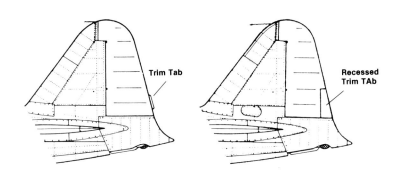

Model 22 (early)  Model 22 (late)

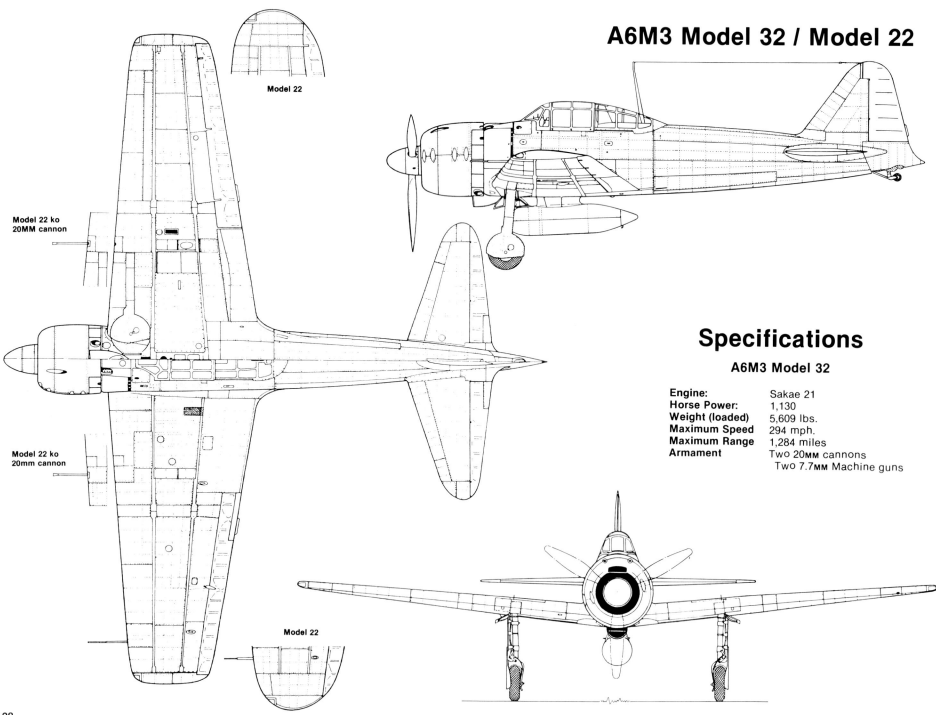

# A6M3 Model 22KO

Model 22　　　　Model 22a

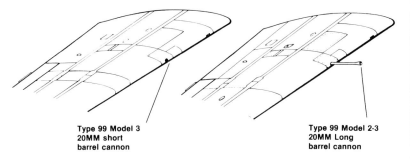

Type 99 Model 3 20MM short barrel cannon

Type 99 Model 2-3 20MM Long barrel cannon

A6M3a Model 22a equipped with the long barrelled 20MM cannon at Rabaul. The smoke in the background is from an active volcano near the airstrip.

A very mysterious A6M3 Model 22 at Rabaul East in mid 1943. The nose and fuselage are very clearly Model 22, but the wing is of the later A6M5 Model 52 design. It is not known if the plane is a field modification or production transition machine.

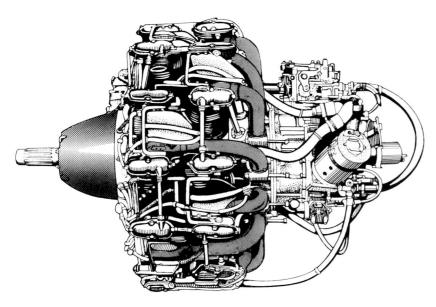

## Najajma Sakae Model 21 (1130 hp) Engine

Carrying tail codes 6-171, this Zero 22 of an unknown unit is seen at Rabaul in late 1943. During the latter half of 1943 the land based units at Rabaul abolished the alpha-numeric tail codes and adopted a completely numerical code system.

Ground maintainence crewmen at Rabaul East take a break. The crewman on the left is holding what looks to be a bottle of saki.

# A6M5 Model 52

In an attempt to meet the new generation of American fighters on more equal terms and to simplify production, the Zero underwent a series of improvements and changes. Based on the Model 32, the short wing span was retained but wing tips were rounded. A heavier gauge metal skin was added to the wings in order to increase diving speed; and to increase maximum speed, the exhaust collector ring was replaced by individual exhaust stacks exiting between redesigned notched cowling flaps. The 12 gallon fuel tanks of the Zero 22 were retained.

The prototype of the A6M5 Model 52, flying for the first time during the summer of 1943, was the first of over 6000 Model 52 variants to be produced, making it the most produced of all the Zero Models. Maximum speed was raised to 351 mph in level flight and the diving speed limit was increased to 410 mph. To replace the huge losses sustained during the fighting for Guadalcanal, the Zero 52 was rushed to the Solomons area as quickly as they were built. What could not be replaced was the huge losses of experienced pilots. And while the Zero 52 could nearly hold its own against the new American F6F Hellcat, if flown by an experienced pilot, experienced pilots were making up a smaller and smaller percentage of the available aircrew.

# A6M5 Model 52 KO

While the Zero 52 was nearly able to match the performance of the 2000 hp F6F Hellcat, its light construction and lack of pilot protection usually meant it fell victim to the Hellcat's heavy fire power. Under the designation A6M5 Model 52 *KO* (A6M5a Model 52a), the 100 round drum-fed type 99 Model 2-3 20MM cannon was replaced with a 125 round belt fed type 99 Model 2-4 20MM cannon and the wing skin was selectively strengthened to increase the diving speed from 410 mph to 460 mph. Deliveries began in March of 1944 with 391 of the *KO* variant being produced by Mitsubishi.

# A6M5 Model 52 OTSU

Built in parallel with the Model 52 *KO* was the A6M5 Model 52 *OTSU* (A6M5b Model 52b). To increase fire power the starboard fuselage mounted 7.7 machine gun was replaced with a type 3 13MM machine gun, the faired housing of which was enlarged and slightly offset to the starboard. A 45MM plate of armored glass was added to the windscreen and an automatic system of CO2 fire extinguishers was installed around the fuselage fuel tank and around the firewall. To increase combat range, provision was made on some 52bs for the installation of a 150 liter drop tank under each wing. 470 Zero 52bs were produced by Mitsubishi and an unknown quantity by Nakajima.

# A6M5 Model 52 HEI

When it was realized that the promised A7M1 Reppu would not be in production, a further update of the Model 52 was made during the late summer of 1944. To satisfy front line demands for increased fire power and pilot protection, most of the changes were made in these areas under the designation A6M5 Model 52 *HEI* (A6M5c Model 52c). Armament was increased by adding a type 3 13MM machine gun with 240 rounds to each wing just outboard of the 20MM cannons. The nose mounted 7.7MM machine gun was deleted. Armament now consisted of five weapons; two wing mounted 20MM cannons, two wing mounted 13MM machine guns and one fuselage mounted 13MM machine gun. This was the heaviest armament configuration yet used on the *Rei-sen* and was used on all subsequent Zero models. On a few of the Model 52cs, the 30/60 kg wing bomb racks were replaced by a rack to carry air-to-air rocket bombs. An 8MM armor plate was installed behind the pilot's seat and a 55MM plate of armored glass was installed behind the pilots head. An additional 37 gallon self-sealing fuel tank was installed behind the pilot's seat.

All of these modifications added nearly 700 additional pounds to the already overloaded 1938 design. The original performance characteristics of the *Rei-sen* fighter no longer existed in the terribly underpowered Zero 52c. Mitsubishi proposed to the Navy that the 1350 hp Mitsubishi *Kinsei* 62 engine, which would provide much needed additional horse power, be installed in the aged airframe. The Navy refused and suggested that the *Sakae* engine be equipped with a water methanol injection. However, development of the water injection system was slow in coming so the Model 52 was powered by the *Sakae* 21. The A6M5 Model 52c flew for the first time in November of 1944 with very disappointing results. Only 93 were produced before production was terminated.

The new individual exhaust pipes replacing the exhaust collector ring helped to increase the Zero 52's maximum speed to 351 mph in level flight. The new exhaust pipes exited between the cowling flaps which were notched.

This A6M5 Model 52 is equipped with a 30/60 kg bomb rack under each wing mounted just outside the landing gear. Note how the Dark Green paint overlaps the wing leading edge.

Based on the Model 32, the wing span was short, but the wing tips were rounded. This Zero 52 of the Omura Detachment of the Sasebo Kokutai at Omura Air Base during the middle of 1944, carries a very unusual unit marking on the tail. The drop tank is a late wooden 330 liter tank with a fin.

This A6M5 Model 52 of the 221st Kokutai is having its 12 gallon port wing tank fueled at Kasanohara Air Base in Kyushu during the summer. The spinner is polished metal and the propeller blades are painted Dark Brown with 50MM wide Yellow/Orange stripes near the tips.

# Cowling Development

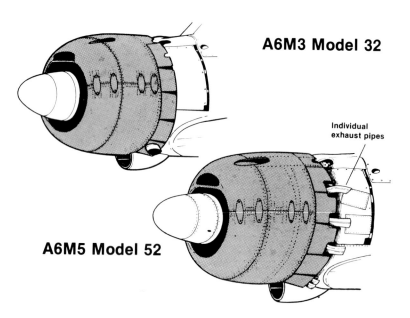

A6M3 Model 32

A6M5 Model 52

Individual exhaust pipes

# Wing Development

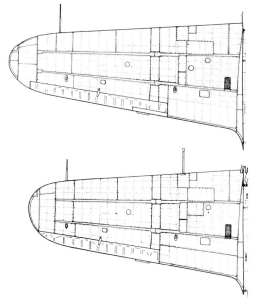

A6M3 Model 22

A6M5 Model 52

A formation of four Model 52s on patrol. The three plane formation was the standard fighting formation of the Japanese Navy during the early part of the war, but from 1944 the four plane formation became standard.

These Zero 52s on Rabaul, belonging to an unknown unit, have had the White outline around the Hinomaru painted over with Black paint.

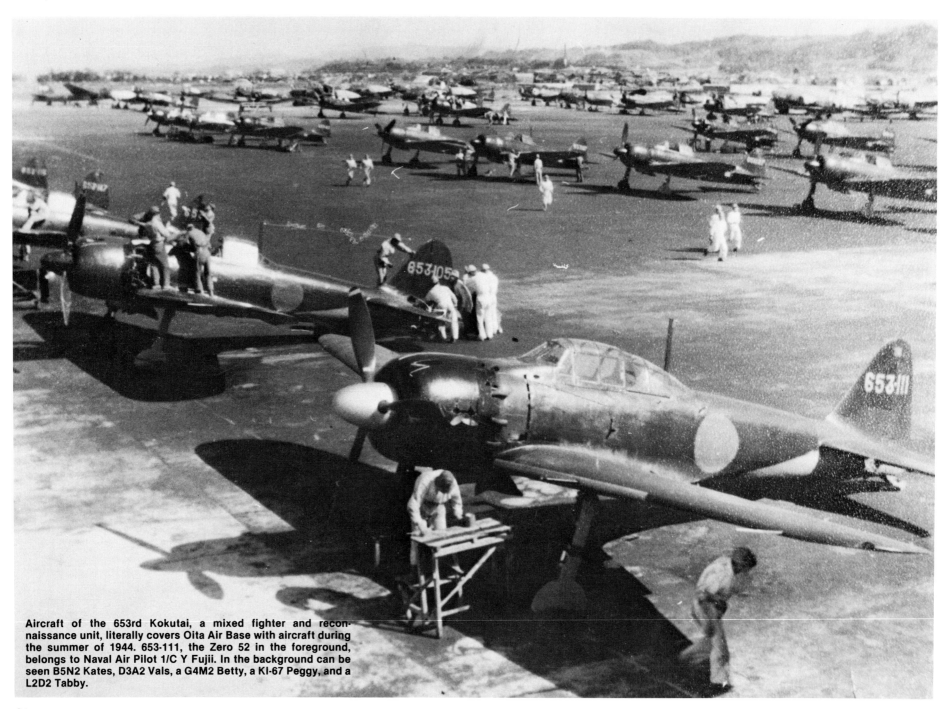

Aircraft of the 653rd Kokutai, a mixed fighter and reconnaissance unit, literally covers Oita Air Base with aircraft during the summer of 1944. 653-111, the Zero 52 in the foreground, belongs to Naval Air Pilot 1/C Y Fujii. In the background can be seen B5N2 Kates, D3A2 Vals, a G4M2 Betty, a KI-67 Peggy, and a L2D2 Tabby.

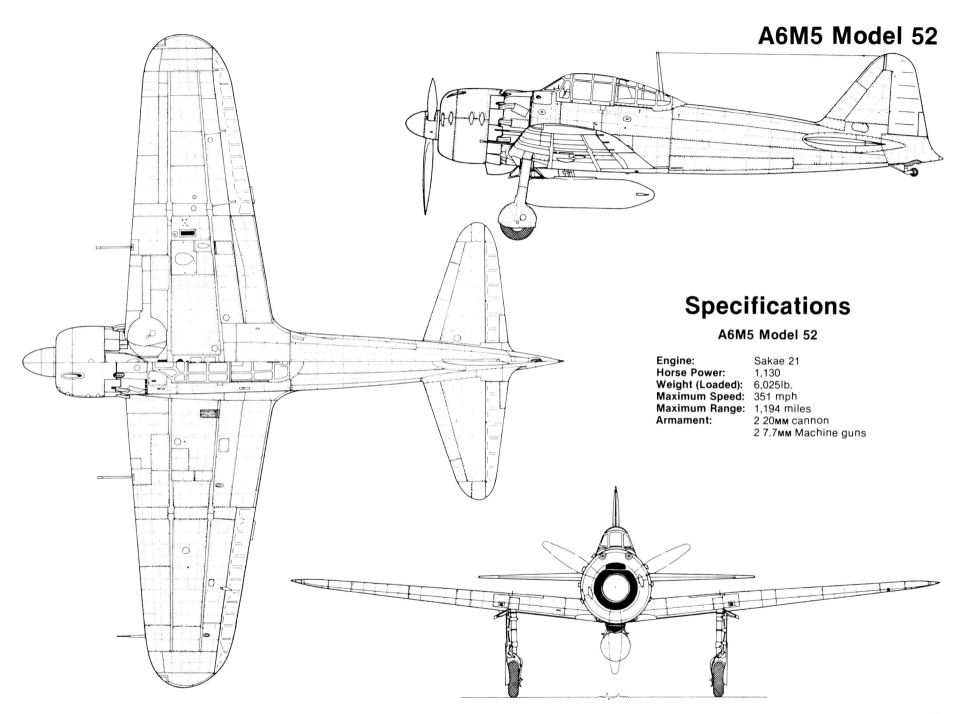

# A6M5 Cockpit

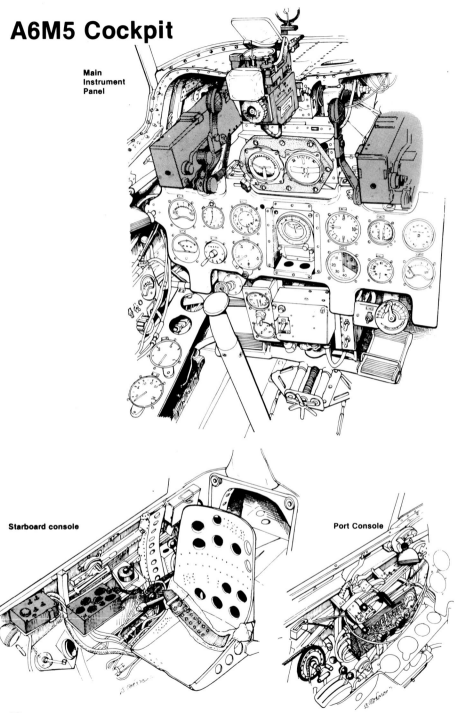

Main Instrument Panel

Starboard console

Port Console

This Zero 52 of the 312th Kokutai, carrying tail codes of 312-122 at Kasumigaura Air Base, has had the tail cone removed. This unit was charged with training "Shusui" rocket fighter pilots as well as local fighter defense.

Few aircraft were as aerodynamically sleek as the Zero. The White tear drop shape in the center of the photo is a navigation light.

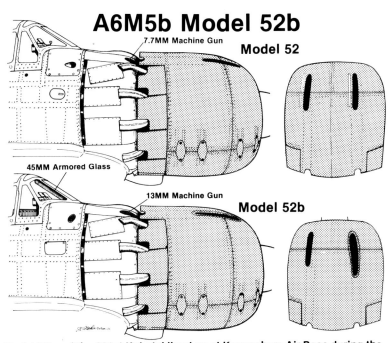

## A6M5b Model 52b

Model 52bs of the 221st Kokutai lined up at Kasanohara Air Base during the spring of 1944. The aircraft in the background carry a D under the tail code identifies it as belonging to the 407th Hikotai, however the meaning of the ZII on the tail of the aircraft in the foreground is unknown.

In this line up of Zero 52bs, the second aircraft from the left is 221-16 ZII. The rarely seen 150 liter wing mounted drop tanks seem to be carried on ZII coded machines only. Note the redesigned shape of the 20mm cannon fairings.

Behind the ground crew "Sumo Wrestlers" is another Z coded Zero 52b equipped with 150 liter drop tanks. The White outline around the fuselage Hinomaru has been over painted with Black paint to present less of a target.

The removal of the 20MM wing cannon allows an excellent view of the new fairing.

## Drop Tank Development

**A6M2 to A6M5**

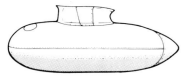

Metal drop tank

**A6M5 to A6M5b**

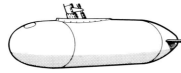

Wooden drop tank

## Wing Armament

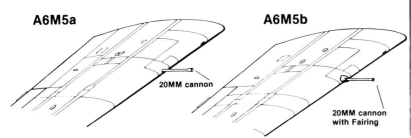

A6M5a — 20MM cannon

A6M5b — 20MM cannon with Fairing

This Model 52 Otsu (Model 52b), TSU-29, belongs to the Tsukuba Kokutai, which was a training group until the B-29 raids forced the pilot instructors to begin carrying out interception missions. The 45MM armored glass added to the windscreen of the b-series is barely visible.

The 302nd Night Fighter Kokutai at Atsugi Air Base during early 1945. The first Hikotai is equipped with both the Zero 52a and Zero 52b, while the second Hikotai is equipped with the J1N3 Gekko, D4Y2-S Suisei and P1Y1 Ginga.

# A6M5c Model 52c Wing Armament

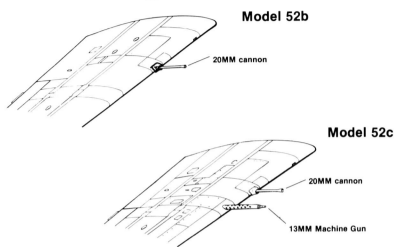

# Drop Tank Development

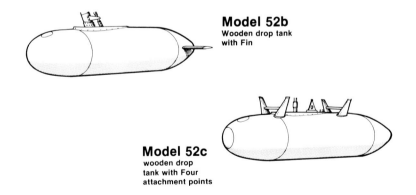

(Above Right) This A6M5c Model 52c of the Yatabe Kokutai is preparing to escort a Kamikaze attack during the U.S. landings on Okinawa. The Zero 52c carried an additional 13mm machine gun mounted in each wing just outboard of the 20mm cannon.

This Model 52c, with its prop and spinner removed at the end of the war, carries the late four attachment point wooden drop tank.

A Zero 52c, of the Yatabe Kokutai, carrying the late style drop tank with four attachment points.

Note the lack of a gas discharge vent in the starboard machine gun access panel where the 7.7 machine gun was removed, which left the Model 52c armed with five weapons. The additional 45MM armored glass plate can be seen attached to the front of the windscreen. Behind the pilot can be seen the 55MM armored glass.

### Armor
### Seat

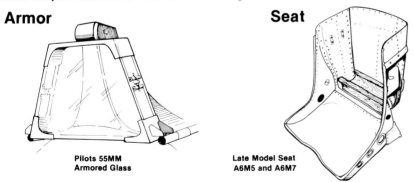

Pilots 55MM Armored Glass

Late Model Seat A6M5 and A6M7

Kill markings on the side of the Zero 52c flown by Naval Air Pilot 1/C Takeo Tanimizu of the 303rd Hikotai, 203rd Kokutai at Kagoshima Air Base during June of 1945. The five U.S. National insignias, with arrows through them, represent five confirmed U.S. Fighters shot down, and the lower insignia, without an arrow, represents a probable kill. Above the fighter kills are two four engine bomber silouettes representing two B-29 kills. T. Tanimizu ended the war with 18 kills. The paint on the fuselage has obviously been brush painted.

## Underwing Bomb Rack

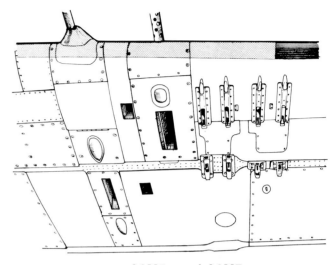

**A6M5c and A6M7**

Armament of the A6M5c Model 52c was increased to five weapons with the addition of two wing mounted 13MM machine guns and the deletion of the 7.7 fuselage mounted machine gun. The late model drop tank with four attachment points is carried. The Dark Green paint toward the end of the war became almost Black Green.

## Wing Rack

**A6M5c and A6M7**

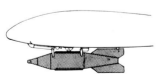

30 kg Bomb

This A6M5c Model 52c has had the wing armament removed, which would indicate that the aircraft is probably a training aircraft. Kasanohara Air Base in late 1944.

# A6M6c Model 53c

The water-methanol *Sakae* 31a engine, originally proposed for the Model 52c, was ready for installation during the fall of 1944. Under the designation A6M6c Model 53c the water-methanol powered fighter was a bitter disappointment. The *Sakae* 31a engine turned out less power than its predecessor and the water-methanol metering system constantly malfunctioned. Only one example of the Zero 53c was produced.

# A6M7 Model 63

The final production version of the *Rei-sen* fighter was built around the finally perfected water-methanol injected 1130 hp *Sakae* 31 engine. The five weapon armament of the Model 52c was retained, but the lower fuselage/center wing section was strengthened so the normal 87 gallon drop tank could be replaced by a 550 lb bomb rack. In order to increase dive bombing speed the tail section was again reinforced with a heavier gauge skin. To increase range, provision was made for the installation of a 150 liter drop tank under each wing.

The prototype of the Model 63 first flew in May of 1945 with production beginning the same month. Because of confusion and the destruction of records at the end of the war, no accurate determination of the number of Model 63s produced has been made. It is known that a number of earlier Models were retrofitted with the dive bombing equipment especially for use as Kamikaze aircraft.

**Equipped with a fuselage rack that was designed to carry either a drop tank or a 550 lb bomb, the A6M7 Model 53 was the first production Rei-sen designed as a fighter/bomber. Going into production in May of 1945, aircraft began appearing over frontlines at the end of the month.**

## Fuselage Bomb Rack

250 kg Bomb

**On the underside of the wing, just outboard of the wing armament (the 13mm machine guns have been removed), are the attachment points for wing bombs.**

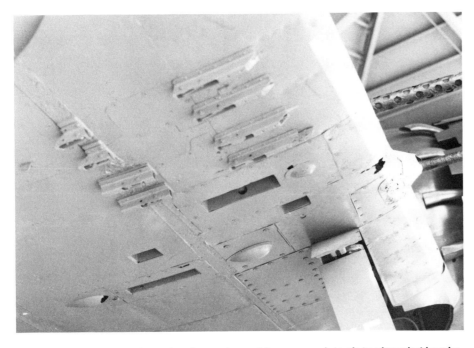

(Above) Besides bombs, the underwing racks could accommodate air-to-air rocket bombs. A few years ago a complete A6M7 Model 63 was found and recovered from Lake Biwa near Kyoto. It is now on display at the Arashiyama Museum.

(Above Right) The skin on the tail surfaces were strengthened to increase the A6M7 Model 63's diving speed.

## A6M7 Type 4 Gunsight

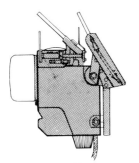
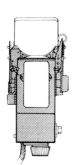

Right Side   Rear View

In order to accommodate the water-methanol injected Sakae 31 powerplant, the cowling of the Model 63 was larger than earlier models and gave the appearance of a very poor fit (which was not the case). The stripes on the landing gear covers are Red, Yellow and Blue, from top to bottom.

# A6M Fighter/Bomber

The very idea of hanging a big, heavy, cumbersome bomb on the Zero was an anathema to the Japanese Navy Air Force. It was only the desperation of the last years of the war that forced the Fighter/Bomber concept on the Japanese. To meet this demand for a Fighter/Bomber, a 250 kg. Bomb rack was designed and retrofitted to service aircraft.

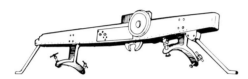

250 kg Bomb Rack

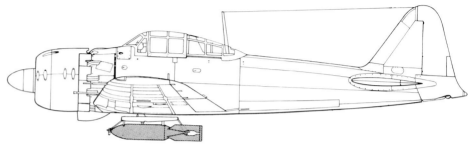

**A6M5 Fighter Bomber**

Believed to be a photo of the first Kamikaze Special Attack of the 201st Kokutai taking off from Mabaracat Air Base in the Philippines on 25 October 1944. Equipped with bomb laden A6M2s and A6M5s, this first Kamikaze unit, "Shinkishima-Tai" was led by Lt Yukio Seki, believed to be flying 02-888. The two Zeros at the far right are carrying drop tanks and are probably escorts for the Kamikazes. This early mission was purely voluntary. Later, pilots were ordered to carry out Kamikaze missions.

# A6M2-K

Developed using obsolete Model 11 airframes, the first example of the Zero trainer was officially accepted by the Navy in March of 1944 under the designation A6M2 Type O Training Fighter Model 11. A two seated dual control trainer, it was used to quickly transition student pilots to the Zero, cutting down both accidents and training time. A long, narrow stability fin was added to the fuselage side just in front of the horizontal stabilizer. The tail wheel was fixed down and a larger diameter tire was added to the tail wheel. The 20MM wing armament was removed as were the main landing gear doors. The radio mast was relocated from the rear of the greenhouse to a position between the front and back seat. Some machines had the tail cone removed as well. A total of 273 A6M2-Ks were produced by Hitachi Co. Some A6M2-K trainers were used for Kamikaze attacks near the end of the war

A long, narrow stability fin was added to the rear of the fuselage. Because of the Zeros construction, the extra seat and extended canopy was easily added without making any structural changes. This machine of the Tsukuba (Training) Kokutai is painted overall Orange with a Black cowling, the Red "No Step" line is visible on the wing.

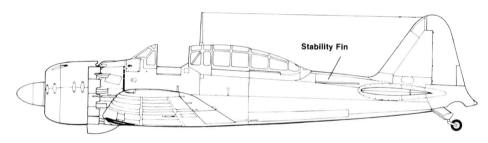

Stability Fin

As American raids on Japan increased during the closing days of the war, training aircraft were repainted in Dark Green and the White outline around the Hinomaru was over painted. Coded 312-406, this A6M2-K Trainer belongs to the 312th Kokutai and is on a training flight over the Kanto Plains during April 1945.

This Orange A6M2-K, coded TSU-403, is serving with the Tsukuba Kokutai during early 1944. The Black paint of the cowling extends diagonally to the windscreen. The radio mast was relocated to a position between the front and back seat. Note the position of the fixed tail wheel.

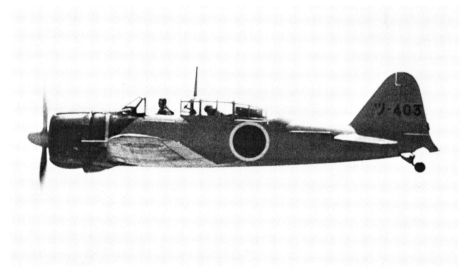

# A6M2-N

Realizing an immediate need for a fighter plane that could operate in remote areas of the Pacific where the construction of airfields was impractical, in late 1940, pending production of the fighter floatplane N1K1 *Kyofu* (code named Rex), the Navy issued 15-*Shi* specifications to Nakajima to develop a floatplane fighter version of the Zero based on the Model 11. Eliminating the undercarriage and retraction mechanism, which was faired over, a unique triangular main strut and two secondary struts were used to mount the single main float; the outrigger floats were mounted on single slender struts. The tail wheel and landing hook were removed and faired over, and to increase lateral stability, a long narrow fin was added to the bottom of the fuselage below the tail assembly and the rudder was extended downward. The cockpit roll bar was deleted.

The 15-*Shi* floatplane flew for the first time on 8 December 1941, the same day OPERATION HAWAII was carried out. Under the designation A6M2 Type 2 Fighter floatplane the Navy accepted the new float fighter in July 1942. A total of 327 A6M2-Ns were produced through September of 1943 when production was terminated. The Allied code name for the A6M2-N was "Rufe".

## Cowling Development

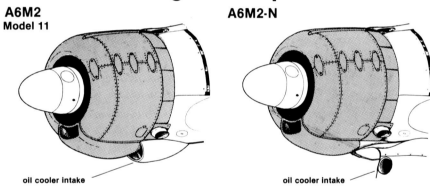

The Model 11 was used as the basis of the 15 Shi floatplane development because it did not have the folding wingtips of the later Model 21. The landing gear, retraction mechanism, tail wheel and tail hook were removed and faired over. A triangular main support and two smaller rear supports attached the float to the fuselage. This unique configuration not only offered high strength but low air drag as well.

The polished metal propeller and spinner are of the early type. The propeller carries Red stripes near the blade tips.

## Tail Development

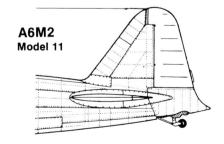
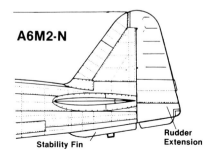

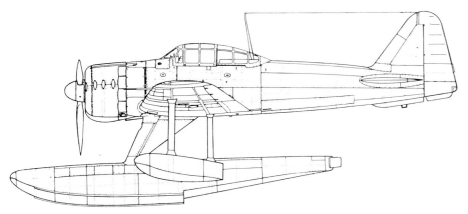

## A6M2-N Float Plane

(Above) This formation of A6M2-N floatplanes, two in Dark Green over Light Gray and two in overall Light Gray with Black cowls, belong to an unknown unit.

(Above Left) To increase lateral stability, the A6M2-N had a long, narrow ventral fin added to the fuselage under the tail section and the lower rudder was extended. This machine, coded Kashi-103, of the Kashima (Training) Kokutai, has Dark Green upper surfaces and Light Gray under surfaces.

A pair of A6M2-Ns of the 802 Kokutai during fleet escort duty in the Marshall Islands on 12 July 1943. 60 kg anti-submarine bombs are carried under each wing. The paint has been worn off the float by constant use.

(Above Right) N1-118, flown by Lt Keizo Yamazaki of the 802nd Kokutai, is painted overall Light Gray with two Medium Blue fuselage bands. The tail stripe, aircraft code and three kill markings are all in Red. 11 February 1943 at Shortland Seaplane Base in the Solomon Islands.

This Dark Green over Light Gray A6M2-N of the 802nd Kokutai at Jaluit Island (Marshall Islands), is being prepared for an anti-submarine patrol. The author's exhaustive research has failed to turn up any evidence that A6M2-N floatplanes were ever painted purple as has been depicted.

Returning from an anti-submarine patrol, this A6M2-N taxis toward shore at Jaluit Island on 10 June 1943.

(Right) Being refueled, this A6M2-N carries its codes, N1-119, in Red with a White outline, the rudder stripe is also Red outlined in White.

Jaluit Seaplane Base was ideally located within a coral reef barrier which provided ideal take off and landing conditions. The third aircraft from the left, coded N1-118, was flown by Lt Yamazaki. 27 May 1943.

# Luftwaffe Aircraft
## From
## squadron/signal publications

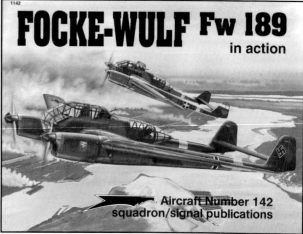